This delightful Fireside book is the latest in a series that have been specially imagined to help grown-ups learn about the world around them. Using large clear type, simple and easy-to-grasp words, frequent repetition, and thoughtful matching of text with pictures, these books should be a great comfort to grown-ups.

The Fireside Grown-up Guides understand that the world is just as confusing to a forty-year-old as it is to a four-year-old. By breaking down the complexity of grown-up life into easy-to-digest nuggets of information, and pairing them with colorful illustrations even a child could under-stand, the Fireside Grown-up Guides prove that being a grown-up can be as simple as "look and remember."

The publishers gratefully acknowledge assistance provided by Josh Weinstein, Egregius Professor of Reference at Mars University and Reader-in-Residence at Springfield Library, in compiling this book.

GUIDE TO

THE

HANGOVER

by

J. A. HAZELEY, N.S.F.W. and J. P. MORRIS, O.M.G.

Authors of *Bedroom Secrets of the Boardroom Batman*

TOUCHSTONE

New York   London   Toronto   Sydney   New Delhi

Sometimes, when we drink too much, we get a hangover.

There is no cure for the hangover, but it can be treated with a cup of strong coffee and a couple of fried breakfasts.

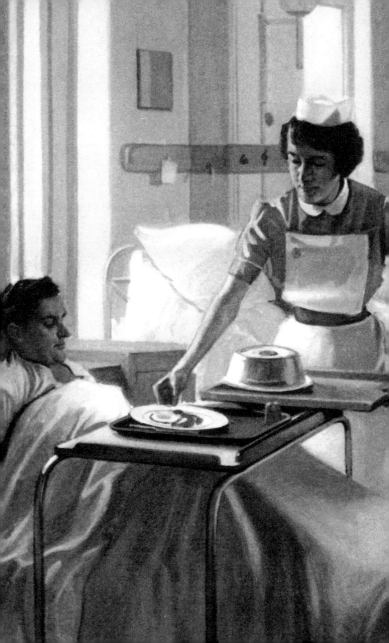

A good hangover should be a total mystery to you.

How did this happen? Why do you feel so ill?

Pretend to yourself that you drank less than you did. Insist you stuck to beer, forgetting the champagne at the start of the evening and the round of jalapeño tequilas you did for a bet in the bar by the freeway ramp at 2 a.m.

Some hangover symptoms are caused by impurities that enter the body along with the alcohol.

These impurities can include methanol, acetone, acetaldehyde, esters, tannins, bags of M&M's, fully loaded Quiznos meatball subs, and Doritos Jacked Ranch Dipped Hot Wings flavored chips.

What a confusing world it can seem with a hangover.

Sit as still as you can. Do not attempt to make any decisions.

Look out the window. Can you recognize simple shapes or colors? Is there a moon or a sun in the sky? What sort of a name might you have? Where might there be bacon?

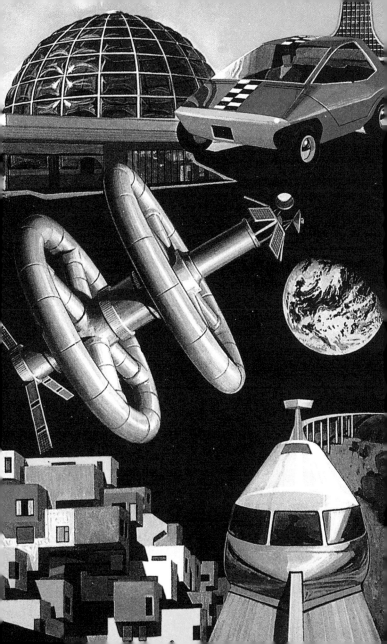

Consuming alcohol lowers the body's reserves of vital elements such as iron, potassium, water, and bacon.

Every unit of alcohol kills the equivalent of two inches of bacon, which must be replaced the next morning.

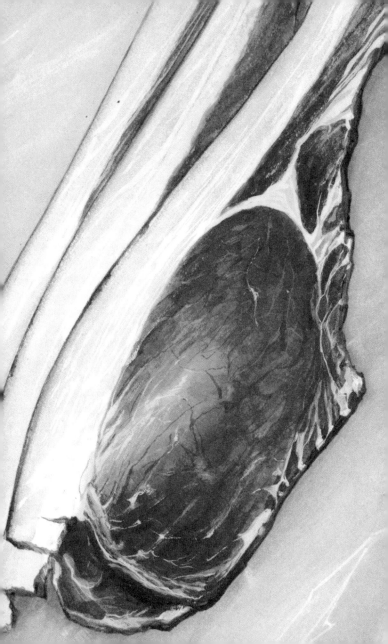

Prepare a hangover first-aid kit of a banana and a pint of water to put by your bedside before going out for an evening's drinking.

When you wake fully dressed the next morning, you can look at the untouched glass and the uneaten banana and wonder who left them there and why.

Peggy is trying "the hair of the dog" to get rid of her hangover.

She was drinking gin last night, so a sip from the gin bottle will help put her body back in balance.

Peggy does not know where the recorder came from. She does remember stealing a street musician's violin case for her cab fare home. Maybe that explains it.

Len's mouth feels like he fell asleep tongue-first on an antique bear pelt. His heart is galloping, his hair aches, and he worries that there is sweat building up underneath his fingernails.

Len has come outside for some fresh air, but now remembers he is scared of fresh air today.

Maybe the policeman can help.

"Can I get you a drink, Len?" asks the policeman.

Michael is bored. Mommy has not moved since she put the DVD on.

The menu screen has been going around and around for two hours. Mommy forgot to press play.

Michael should not have woken poor Mommy up so early.

Friday night work drinks went on longer than expected. Ron has a head like a smelting plant full of howler monkeys on ephedrine.

Ron is glad Saturday mornings require little more than the vocabulary, reasoning, and motor skills of a seven-year-old. Ron is happy on the floor.

Later, he will try to buy a head of garlic at a self-service checkout and will burst into tears.

The morning after the party, Emeric is woken by a stray cat licking his face. He has slept under a hedge and cannot remember a thing.

Emeric uses street signs and clues from his clothing to piece together where he lives and what he does for a living.

Emeric hopes it was a theme party. If these are his work clothes, no wonder he needed to drink.

The morning after a wedding, everybody feels a little the worse for wear.

It can seem like there are no grown-ups left in charge. What will happen? Who will help us? Is this the end? What if Earth crashes into the sun?

Do not panic. Soon the hangover will be over, and you can all celebrate with a nice drink.

Going to work with a hangover might seem impossible, but it is important that you do not lose your job. Even if that was the reason you got drunk.

Try to turn up at the usual time, say hello to everyone, then have a little nap somewhere quiet, such as the roof.

What's the worst that could happen?

Harold knows the best way to avoid a hangover is to remember how bad he felt the last time he drank too much wine.

Sadly, after the first glass of wine, Harold remembers feeling quite good. And the next glass makes him feel even better.

"I feel invincible," roars Harold.

Try not to drive or operate heavy machinery with a hangover.

Last night, Bernie and his crew celebrated winning the company football pool.

Now they are going to have to build this part of the hospital again.

Susan woke up next to a full glass of wine. She left it by the bedside in case she became thirsty in the night.

Now Susan does not know whose apartment she's in or where the nearest train station might be.

At least she is dressed properly in case there is another party on the walk home.

This cat is judging you.

Get off the floor.

And put some underwear on.

If you are drinking something unfamiliar, be prepared for it to affect you in unexpected ways.

The distillation acts of the seventeenth century introduced gin to many British towns for the first time.

This is Canterbury.

Tony took $200 out from the cash machine after work. He woke up drenched in sweat with loose change all over his bed.

Tony hopes the many, many coins will be enough to go and buy an important breakfast.

Tony has thirty-five cents.

Most stores offer refunds for purchases you discover you made while drunk as long as you keep the packaging and receipt.

For younger people, a hangover's symptoms are mainly physical.

The body is listless, the head is sore; they crave food for no reason and spend a long time in the bathroom.

For older people, this is perfectly normal. So for them, a hangover is more spiritual.

The morning after consuming alcohol, you may find you are more sensitive to noise.

Some people can actually "see" sounds. It is almost as if drinking gives you superpowers!

While the effect wears off, remember, you do not have to get out of the way of birdsong, or duck when someone calls your name.

There are lots of ways to avoid a hangover.

Try vomiting regularly into a bag. Put a brick on the bag and keep vomiting until the bag is full enough to tip it over.

Or set yourself limits. Try drinking only what you can get into your body without touching the container. This is also a good way of turning drinking from a chore into a game.

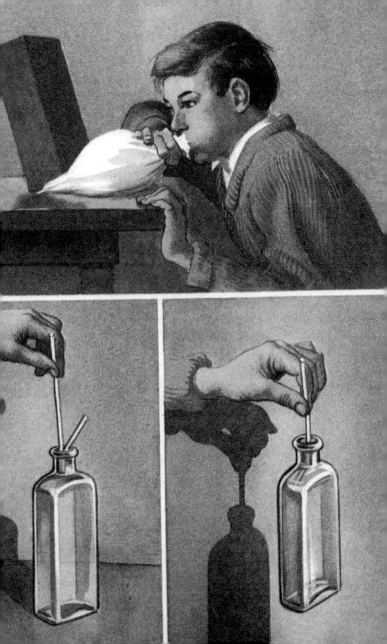

Winston Churchill was prime minister of Britain from 1940 to 1945 and again from 1951 to 1955. He was First Lord of the Admiralty in the Great War, won the Nobel Prize in Literature, and led the Allies to defeat Nazi Germany in the Second World War.

He had a persistent, nagging hangover from 1892 to 1965, when he died.

He never surrendered.

TOUCHSTONE
An Imprint of Simon & Schuster, Inc.
1230 Avenue of the Americas
New York, NY 10020

First Touchstone hardcover edition October 2016

TOUCHSTONE and colophon are registered trademarks of Simon & Schuster, Inc.

For information about special discounts for bulk purchases,
please contact Simon & Schuster Special Sales at 1-866-506-1949
or business@simonandschuster.com.

The Simon & Schuster Speakers Bureau can bring authors to your live event.
For more information or to book an event, contact the Simon & Schuster Speakers Bureau
at 1-866-248-3049 or visit our website at www.simonspeakers.com.

Manufactured in Mexico

1   3   5   7   9   10   8   6   4   2

Library of Congress Cataloging-in-Publication Data

Names: Hazeley, Jason, author. | Morris, Joel (Comedy writer), author.
Title: The Fireside grown-up guide to the hangover / J.A. Hazeley and J. B. Joel Morris.
Other titles: Ladybird book of the hangover | Hangover
Description: New York : Touchstone, [2016] | Series: The Fireside grown-up guides
Identifiers: LCCN 2016011237 | ISBN 9781501150715 (hardback)
Subjects: LCSH: Hangover--Humor. | Hangover cures--Humor. | BISAC: HUMOR /
Topic / Adult.
Classification: LCC PN6231.H34 H39 2016 | DDC 818/.602--dc23
LC record available at https://lccn.loc.gov/2016011237

ISBN 978-1-5011-5071-5
ISBN 978-1-5011-5072-2 (ebook)

THE ARTISTS

Robert Ayton
John Berry
G. Cansdale
Frank Humphris
John Kenney
Jorge Nuñez
B. H. Robinson
G. Robinson
Harry Wingfield
Eric Winter
Gerald Witcomb

THE FIRESIDE GROWN-UP GUIDES TO

MINDFULNESS

THE HUSBAND

THE MOM

THE HANGOVE

If you benefited from the Fireside Grown-up Guide in your hand, look for these others wherever produce and ductwork are sold:

THE HUSBAND

The husband knows many things. For example, he knows how many stairs there are, in case he arrives home unable to see them properly.

MINDFULNESS

Alison has been staring at this beautiful tree for five hours. She was meant to be in the office. Tomorrow she will be fired. In this way, mindfulness will have solved her work-related stress.

THE MOM

The mom does not like hearing her own voice. That is because it does not sound like her voice anymore. It sounds like her mom's.